GRAYS THURROCK DISTRICT

DISTRICT

A Pictorial History

Including Aveley, Baker Street, Chadwell St Mary, Corringham,
Corytown, Fobbing, Grays, Horndon-on-the-Hill, North and
South Ockendon, Orsett, Purfleet, Stanford-le-Hope, North and
South Stifford, Thurrock and Tilbury.

An engraving of the entrance to Tilbury Fort, published in 1818.

GRAYS THURROCK DISTRICT
A Pictorial History

Including Aveley, Baker Street, Chadwell St Mary, Corringham, Corytown, Fobbing, Grays, Horndon-on-the-Hill, North and South Ockendon, Orsett, Purfleet, Stanford-le-Hope, North and South Stifford, Thurrock and Tilbury.

Barry Barnes

Phillimore

1988

Published by
PHILLIMORE & CO. LTD.
Shopwyke Hall, Chichester, Sussex

ISBN 0 85033 660 0

Printed and bound in Great Britain by
BIDDLES LTD.
Guildford, Surrey

For Sheila
Thanks for everything

List of Illustrations

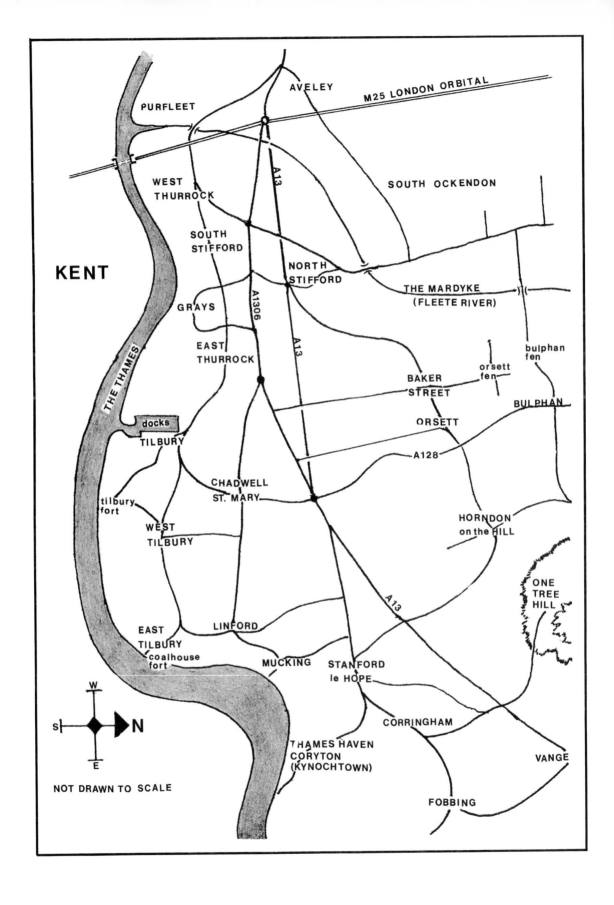

Introduction

Grays Thurrock, an area of some 65 square miles, is situated in south Essex. The River Thames forms its southern border whilst the outer fringes of east London touch the west side of the borough as does the urban sprawl of Basildon on the east. Thurrock is a region of diverse countryside: in the south is low-lying marshland, in the north the land rises steeply at the foot of the Langdon Hills, and the heart of the area comprises a mixture of rich farm-land and fens.

A beauty spot known as One Tree Hill affords a fine view of the district south towards the Thames. To the right, in the extreme west, are the 'Ockendons', originally a number of farms and smallholdings strung together by the villages of North and South Ockendon along with Aveley. These villages have almost been swallowed up by 'new' estates built to accommodate the homeless of London after the last war. Some rural pockets still exist, namely the village green at South Ockendon where stands the village church dedicated to St Nicholas. This church has a fine round tower built in the 13th century, one of very few in the country. Also on the green is the *Royal Oak* which can be dated back to the 15th century. North Ockendon is a good example of a largely unspoilt Essex village and the High Street buildings above the modern shop-fronts at Aveley indicate what it must have looked like over a century ago.

Between One Tree Hill and the 'Ockendons' is the village of Bulvan, now spelt Bulphan. Bulvan means fortified fen and consists of acres of arable and cattle grazing land interspersed with groups of houses and smallholdings. Running through Bulvan fen is the Mardyke, a small river that acts as a drainage ditch for the land it cuts across. Specially designed barges once used the Mardyke to reach the farms on the fen. Bulvan village, which is now cut in two by the A128 trunk road, still has a number of noteworthy artefacts. Apart from the church of St Mary's, there are two cast-iron pumps protected by their own little houses.

To the south of Aveley is Purfleet, a village where legend has it Queen Elizabeth I climbed a hill and, looking down at her navy at anchor being tossed by a storm, said, 'Oh my poor fleet'. In fact the name Purfleet is derived from 'the fleot (stream) of Purta'. This is a reference to the Mardyke that joins the Thames here. Today Purfleet is a highly industrialised area favoured by many large national companies, Esso Petroleum being one of them. Purfleet was chosen as the site for the northern end of the river crossing for the M25 London Orbital Motorway and is now becoming known as the gateway to East Anglia.

Purfleet's near neighbour is West Thurrock. Today it is impossible to see where one finishes and the other starts but within living memory West Thurrock was an entirely separate village dominated by agriculture. Today it is mostly industrial and factories have spread along the river's edge. The power station and Proctor & Gamble's soap factory now dwarf the historic St Clement's church that once stood alone on the marshes and offered a safe resting place for pilgrims who were waiting to cross the river on their way to Canterbury.

Further along the London road is South Stifford. This too was once an entirely separate community, self-sufficient with its own farms, school, shops, bakery and dairy. North Stifford is its rich relation. A sprawling village with a mixture of both old and new, the old consists of the 12th-century church of St Mary the Virgin and a number of thatched cottages plus Coppid Hall which was built in the middle of the 18th century. At the opposite end of the village street to the church a sprinkling of private and council houses in Clockhouse Lane. This road perpetuates the memory of the clockhouse where Sir Thomas Gourney, Sheriff of Essex in 1622, once lived. The house stood where the *Dog and Partridge* now offers refreshment. Outside the village is what remains of the old Stifford Heath, now the grounds of Ardale School which was once known as the Stepney Homes. At the bottom of the hill across the Mardyke is Ford Place, a house that dates back to the middle of the 17th century and has fine plaster ceilings and wood wall panelling. It was recently destroyed in a fire started by vandals.

After South Stifford the London road runs into Grays or Grays Thurrock as it should properly be called. The name is derived from the granting of the manor of Thurrock to Henry de Grey in 1194. Thurrock is thought to come from the Saxon word 'Turroc' meaning the bottom part of a ship where all the filth gathers, and refers to the bend in the river where Grays is located and the tide deposits its flotsam. Grays is now a large rather shabby town, spoilt in the name of modernisation. Here once was a very pretty 'olde worlde' working port. It had a High Street rich in weather-boarded buildings, houses, public houses such as the *Crown and Anchor* and the *White Hart*. Here too were lodging houses for the crews of barges that worked out of the port and the 'Old Dutch House' which was the birth place of the Grays Co-operative Society.

Grays had many other fine buildings including the Carnegie Free Library, Grays Fire Station, the *Queens Hotel* and the *Bull Inn* which, together with most of the old High Street buildings, were all demolished during redevelopment.

Taking the old Tilbury road out of Grays, one passes through Little Thurrock. Very little remains of the old village, the most notable buildings being the church of St Mary and the old school house with its fine clock tower. These border the village green, whilst just along the road is the *Bull Inn* along with a number of ancient cottages once occupied by farm labourers. In the parish of Little Thurrock, within the area known as Socketts Heath, is Hangman's Wood. In this wood are the curious Daneholes. This should be pronounced Denehole and is derived from the word 'dene' meaning pig pasture. The holes dug in this early pasture have puzzled man for many years. Some feel they were used for storage or hiding places, others believe they were dug to excavate chalk or flints.

The road from Little Thurrock drops gently down to marshes across which is Tilbury. From the edge of the marsh can be seen the dockside cranes and the funnels of the ships being worked in the docks a couple of miles distant. The docks were opened in 1886 and are now an important port of call for the giant container ships that come up the Thames. Both docks and town have seen many changes over the last hundred years. The size of the dock has increased considerably and the town has grown from virtually nothing. There are no really old buildings in Tilbury. The oldest which bears the name Tilbury is Tilbury Fort and is in fact in the parish of West Tilbury. There has been a fortification on this site, a few hundred yards downstream from the present ferry, for many hundreds of years. Many of the buildings standing today were built in the 17th century – for example, the very ornate Water Gate was completed in 1682. About one hundred yards to the west of the fort is a public house called the *World's End*, a fitting name when it was first given over a century ago. From near this spot a ferry has crossed the river for hundreds of years and the old *World's End* is where its passengers waited for the ferryman.

The road from the *World's End* to West Tilbury village is the same road that the ferry passengers and soldiers from the fort would have used. It twists and turns across the low-lying marshland and enters West Tilbury up Gun Hill. Many fine buildings still stand in West Tilbury, the most outstanding being the church dedicated to St James. Although now redundant, it is to be preserved as a private residence. It is in this church that Fairfax, the Roundhead general, when travelling from Maidstone to lay siege to Colchester in 1648, allowed his men to camp and stable their horses. Pews and other wooden furniture are said to have fuelled their camp fires. Here too, in the fields beyond the church, Queen Elizabeth I is said to have delivered her famous rallying speech at the time of the Armada threat in 1588.

Further east down river is East Tilbury, known today for the Bata shoe factory and the huge housing estate that was built to accommodate its workers. In Henry VIII's time it was the site chosen for a blockhouse. Over the years the blockhouse or fort has been much altered and added to. The most recent large-scale rebuilding scheme was undertaken by General Gordon in 1861. The fort is now being restored and will house a military museum. Within yards of Coalhouse Fort stands St Katherine's church. The church has no tower, as it was destroyed by cannon fire from Dutch warships which ventured up the Thames in 1667. The village of East Tilbury has little left of real antiquity due to mass demolition and alteration.

The other side of the level crossing at East Tilbury station is Linford. This hamlet was once called Muckingford but it was rechristened when land developers chose the area in the late 1800s as a site for luxury housing. On the corner of the road that links Chadwell St Mary with Linford stands a house and a single-storey building which looks like a large garage. This was Motts Forge where General Fairfax had his horses reshod while on his journey to Colchester. Opposite the forge is the *George and Dragon* public house, the second building of the same name on this site.

Little remains of the old village of Chadwell St Mary, built on a crossroads. On one corner is Sleepers Farm farmhouse, which has stood here for some 500 years and witnessed many changes. The most momentous occurred in the last half of this century when the fields surrounding the village were chosen for a new housing estate. During the building operations most of the old houses and shops which were the nucleus of the village were swept away. The village does still possess a fine Norman church dedicated to St Mary, in which many ecclesiastical treasures are preserved. Both Sleepers Farm and St Mary's church are built on the very edge of the escarpment that overlooks the marshland and Tilbury beyond. A traveller taking the road down Chadwell Hill towards Tilbury could be forgiven for missing the hamlet of Little Biggin. At the bottom of the hill a road leads to the left and appears to be little more than a farm track. Within a few hundred yards are the dozen or so houses that make up 'Biggin'. Today the road finishes just beyond the last house but it is believed that before the modern surface was laid a track crossed the countryside to emerge at Gun Hill in West Tilbury. Another track on the left, known as Sandy Lane, joins Muckingford Road just beyond Chadwell church. A mile or so along Muckingford Road towards Linford is a large farm, owned by the Cole family for many years. The farm once had a very fine windmill.

A right-hand turning from Linford takes the traveller to Mucking. Beyond the level crossing on the edge of the village is Mucking Hall and then the old *Crown Inn*. Opposite Mucking Hall is the now redundant St John the Baptist church. In the corner of the churchyard is a very fine example of a church schoolhouse, now alas in a very dilapidated condition. To the left of the churchyard is the vicarage. The parish of Mucking contains a number of fine buildings, including St Cleres Hall which is situated at Mucking's northern boundary near Rookery Corner. This was once a very busy road junction. Before the new A13 trunk road was built, the old A13 used to pass within yards of the immaculate lawns of St Cleres Hall. Here too the roads from Horndon-on-the-Hill and Stanford-le-Hope spilled their traffic onto the old London to Southend road. Since the opening of the new road, Rookery Corner has become a local backwater.

From Rookery Corner, Stanford-le-Hope is but a stone's throw away, a sprawling mass of houses and shops covering an area far larger than the original village. The magnificent church of St Margaret of Antioch dominates the hill on which it is built. On top of the hill is the Green although no village green as such now exists. This was once the hub of the village: beside the Green stood the *Cock and Magpie Inn*, the blacksmith's shop, the post office, the doctor's house and other shops necessary for everyday living. Some still stand in another guise, others have been lost forever. St Margaret's church stands beside the Green opposite the site of the old *Cock and Pie*. Looking more like a cathedral than a village church, its foundations date back to Norman times, though it has been altered and rebuilt many times down the ages. The most recent large undertaking was started in 1877 when the 17th-century brick tower was demolished because it was in danger of falling down. The present tower was built a few years later.

The most famous resident of Stanford-le-Hope was the author Joseph Conrad. He took up residence in Ivy Walls, an Elizabethan farmhouse in Billet Lane, in 1897. His son Boris was born in the same house in 1898 and here too he completed his novel *The Black Narcissus*.

From the Green roads run in all directions: one leads down to the new town centre, another threads its way across country to the once busy Stanford-le-Hope wharf, and another leads to Corringham. Corringham, like Stanford-le-Hope, has been greatly enlarged in recent years with new housing estates and a shopping centre, but the old village remains very picturesque and retains much of its old world charm. The *Bull Inn* with parts dating back over 500 years, the Norman church dedicated to St Mary and other weather-boarded houses, all add character to this remnant of old England. At the end of the village street is Corringham Hall Farm where even today farmer Young uses living horsepower on his land in preference to tractors, and old-fashioned threshing and baling machines can still be seen at work.

A steep hill leads from Corringham to Fobbing. From the top of the hill can be seen the *White Lion*, parts of which date back to the 15th century. Attached to the inn is a large room which was once a sail loft, where sails were made and repaired for the many hundreds of Thames sailing barges which visited Fobbing Wharf. The creek which fed the wharf was stopped up after the 1953 east coast floods; originally the water came up to within yards of the bottom of the hill. A number of important buildings still stand in the area, including Fobbing Hall, parts of which date back to the 16th century. There is also a short row of cottages which were once the *Ship Inn*. This may have been the inn referred to by Charles Dickens in *Great Expectations*. It was here that the crews of the barges moored in the creek and the workers from the local brickfields took their refreshments. Fobbing is the village where the Peasants Revolt germinated and the ill-fated march on London began in 1381. St Michael's church, which overlooks the wharf and is a landmark for miles around, has parts dating back to the 13th century. The 15th-century tower affords magnificent views of the Thames Estuary and the rolling hills of Kent beyond. Oil refineries and scores of storage tanks now cover hundreds of acres of the marshland. The area now known as

Coryton was once called Kynochtown, which was created in 1895 when Kynoch and Company bought Borley Farm, a 200-acre site on the desolate marshes. Kynoch's built a massive munitions factory to supply the needs of the government should the expected war in South Africa break out. When war was declared in 1899 the Kynoch factory produced many thousands of tons of explosives. With the factory came workers, so houses, shops, a post office, an institute and a school were soon built. The Corringham Light Railway was laid in 1901 and the village of Kynochtown was joined to the small station at Corringham. Kynoch's factory closed in January 1919.

Leaving Fobbing along Vange Road, the traveller passes a mixture of old and new buildings before joining the A13 trunk road at Vange. Travelling west along the A13 he soon reaches the new junction for Horndon-on-the-Hill. Horndon still retains many of its old buildings, one of the best being the 16th-century woolmarket, a reminder of the village's past wealth. The *Bell Inn* keeps up the quaint custom of nailing a hot cross bun to the beams in the bar every Good Friday. In March 1555 Thomas Higbed was burned at the stake behind this hostelry for denouncing the Catholic faith.

West of Horndon-on-the-Hill is Orsett, approached by a very narrow road more suited to a horse and cart than modern vehicles. Along Orsett Road are a number of brick-built cottages. These once housed agricultural workers, but many are now privately owned. Almost at the end of Orsett Road is Orsett Fruit Farm, once part of the Orsett Estate Company and a reminder of the days when Orsett had many acres of orchards. Good cider could once be purchased at the 'old fruit farm'. On the edge of the village itself, behind a high red-brick wall, is Orsett Hall, once the home of Col. Sir Francis Whitmore, Lord Lieutenant of Essex. The house is now used as an hotel. Orsett has many fine buildings and reminders of its past. At the junction of Pound Lane and the High Road is the village cage or lock up which was rescued from a local farm where it was being used as a chicken house. Beside the cage is the village pound, once used to hold straying cattle until their owners claimed them. Until a few years ago the village still had a working smithy, where one could watch the blacksmith making horseshoes or repairing farming implements. Mr. Fryett was well known as Orsett's blacksmith for many years and was famous for his ornamental wrought-iron work.

Along the High Road from Orsett is the hamlet of Baker Street, sitting sleepily on a crossroads. This was once a busy place – within living memory a healthy milling business operated here. The fine smock windmill is now being renovated and a 17th-century Mill House still stands. A number of fine buildings have been lost over the years including a short row of weather-boarded cottages which once stood adjacent to Mill House along Stifford Road and were perhaps the homes of workers at the mill. Two more rows of cottages, namely Saunders and Lindsey's Cottages, along with a shop known as 'Nellies', all of which stood on the west side of Baker Street, have been lost to the bulldozer.

It is hoped that the pictures which follow may revive many long-forgotten memories of this part of Essex.

Industry

Thurrock has for many years had a great deal of industry, especially along its river front. In the past many tons of chalk have been quarried and many thousands of bricks have been made in the various brickfields across the area. Companies to have favoured Thurrock include Thames Board Mills, Proctor & Gamble, Van den Berghs & Jurgens, Esso and Shell, as well as numerous smaller national and local concerns. Windmills could once be seen all across the Borough and the docks at Tilbury have given employment in the area for some 100 years.

1. Staff of the Box Department at Jurgens margarine works in about 1920. Jurgens, a Dutch company, came to Thurrock in 1918 and produced the new butter substitute. They joined forces with their rivals in 1927 to become Van den Berghs & Jurgens.

2. Thurrock is pockmarked with worked-out quarries. This picture shows some of the men who helped produce this lunar landscape. W. R. Menlove published this postcard. Life for quarry workers must have been hard in the days when a pick, shovel, muscle and sweat were the order of the day.

3. A line-up of early petrol-driven delivery vehicles owned by Seabrooke & Sons. Seabrooke's established their brewery in 1799 and traded as Thorrock Brewery for many years from their premises in Bridge Road, Grays. The company had many public houses all over Essex and north Kent, but was taken over by Charringtons in 1929.

4. Launderers to King George V, Stanford-le-Hope Laundry had premises in London Road. Horse-drawn vans were used to collect and deliver the laundry. This postcard, postmarked Kensington 1913, reads 'will you please arrange with the railway company to collect basket of linen on Friday morning from 8 Princes Gate Knightsbridge'. The Laundry closed down in 1978.

5. Stacey's Garage was one of the first to open in Stanford-le-Hope. Situated in Southend Road, it started as a cycle shop. Advertisements in the shop window show they also sold A.J.S. motorcycles. The event pictured here is not known but it could have been a coronation celebration.

6. Thames Haven ambulance. The London & Thames Haven Oil Company, knowing the danger of working with petroleum and accepting their isolation on the marshes between Corringham and the Thames, set up their own medical team. This picture shows their fine Ford ambulance soon after delivery to the plant some time before 1914.

7. Purfleet's riverside was chosen by many companies as a site for their works. The Anglo-American Oil Company now known as Esso chose the area for a refinery. Here S.S. *Iroquois* is seen tied up at their jetty. The *Iroquois* regularly crossed the Atlantic towing the barge *Narvaho* laden with crude oil from the American oil fields.

8. The massive coal works at Purfleet. Hundreds of ships and barges once called at jetties here to discharge their cargoes of coal brought down from the coalmines in the north. Note the four giant cranes on the waterside and the line of railway trucks across the centre of the picture. The card is postmarked 1915.

9. Chalk was for many years a very important commodity in Purfleet. This picture, postmarked 1916, was taken on the floor of one of the quarries and gives a good idea how large they were – the cliff to the left must be some 50 feet high. Scores of horses were employed pulling wagons along many miles of railway lines.

THAMES PAPER
COMPANY
Lᵀᴰ

PURFLEET

ESSEX

FROM THE AIR.

10. Another firm to set up home at Purfleet was the Thames Paper Company, later Thames Board Mills. Occupying a vast area, they gave employment to hundreds of local men and women. In its heyday one could see rows of barges being towed along the Thames to this factory with their cargoes of waste paper.

11. A good promotional picture issued by Stephens & Carter of London showing their scaffolding work on silos at West Thurrock. They may perhaps have been built for the Tunnel Cement Company.

12. Tilbury early this century was a fast developing town. The newly-opened docks brought many more residents to the area, so there was a great demand for new houses. This picture, taken on 10 May 1929, shows the carpenters and joiners of Tilbury Housing No. 4 section taking time out for a photograph during building work on the new estate.

13. Tilbury Docks about 70 years ago. The cargoes being handled include timber, sacks of grain and bales of wool. The ship being unloaded in the foreground is the *Malakand*, registered in Liverpool. Her cargo is being loaded onto lighters for towing by Thames barge up the river to London.

14. In a dock the size of Tilbury many administrative departments were required to ensure its smooth running. This is the Board of Trade Mercantile Marine office in the dock about 1912.

15. Although Tilbury was fast developing into a busy town, life was still very rural for some. Reed & March's Poultry Farm at Tilbury, shown here early in the century, was situated on the outskirts of the town.

16. This smock mill at South Ockendon, part of Hall Farm, dates back to *c*.1829. The mill and other farm buildings stood next to the moat and water from the moat was fed under the mill to a waterwheel. This waterwheel powered the mill when there was insufficient wind to turn the sails. Last worked in 1923, it collapsed on 2 November 1977.

59719. HORNDON ON THE HILL

17. A post mill stood 50 yards from the church at Horndon until 1917. Built early in the 19th century, it changed hands several times. It was sold in 1857 for £630 and let to Eleazer Tyrrell, a local shopkeeper, for £45 p.a. It was last worked about 1898 by Robert Linn. Only part of the roundhouse stands today.

18.   A rare photograph of the smock mill at West Tilbury, postmarked 1909. This was an outstanding windmill with a tarred roundhouse and weatherboarding with white painted doors, windowframes and cap. The sails and tailwheel must also have been painted white. The picture shows that the mill had a steam engine attached which could be used when the wind dropped.

19.   The smock mill at Baker Street, Orsett, was built towards the end of the 18th century. The machinery could be driven by the steam engine beside the mill if necessary. It operated until about 1916 when gales caused damage amounting to £900 which could not be raised. Lightning destroyed two of the sails in 1926.

20.   Aveley windmill was removed in about 1916 but stood near the Mill House in Mill Road. The Mill House, built in a hollow to avoid taking wind from the sails, still stands and is seen in this picture, postmarked 1903.

21.   Built in the 1870s, Boormans Mill in Stanford-le-Hope once stood on the north side of London Road. This steam-driven mill worked for many years grinding grain from local farms. It closed in 1964.

The River

The River Thames forms Thurrock's southern boundary. It has been used by residents of the area since time began, for transport, as a source of power or food, for recreation and even as a sewer. Within living memory Thames barges used it as their highway to London and training ships such as the *Exmouth, Shaftesbury* and *Cornwall* could be seen moored just off shore.

22. Launched in 1815, the training ship *Cornwall* was positioned close to the *Royal Hotel*, Purfleet, from 1868 to 1928. In September 1915 tragedy struck the ship. An officer and 26 boys were run down by a government tug whilst on a training exercise. The instructor and 16 boys were drowned. They are buried at St Clements, West Thurrock.

23. Built in 1854, the training ship *Shaftesbury* came to Grays in 1878. Up to 400 boys aged between 11 and 14 years were accommodated on board. The boys were trained for service in the Royal Navy or Mercantile Marine. Closed in 1905, she was beached and broken up in 1907.

24. Boys from poor families were trained on board the *Warspite* for a life in the Royal Navy. In 1905, 100 of the boys sailed to Australia on the three-masted barque, *Port Jackson*. The trip took 120 days.

Warspite off Grays.

118792

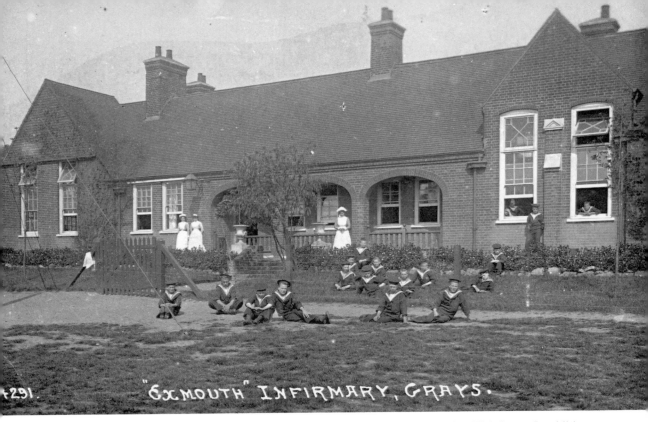

"EXMOUTH" INFIRMARY, GRAYS.

+291.

25.   The training ships' hospital was situated in West Field, an area to the west of the Old High Street. In addition to wards and nursing staff to administer medical care, there was in the grounds a fresh water swimming pool.

26.   Early this century Thurrock's riverside was a favourite mooring place for training ships. The *Exmouth* is still remembered affectionately by locals. This close-up view of the ship that made this shoreline her home in 1905 shows what a fine ship she was. Hundreds of boys were trained for a life in the navy aboard the *Exmouth*. She was removed in 1939.

27. Boys on the *Exmouth* were encouraged to produce costume dramas. This picture, taken by Smith of Grays, shows the players in one such production. Set possibly at the time of the Spanish Armada, much work was put into the costumes and weapons. The ship's deck and superstructure were ideal for such scenes.

28. Group photograph on board T.S. *Exmouth*, taken by Edwin of Grays. This may be a winning rowing team with their instructor.

29. The beach at Grays was opened on 30 July 1906 on the instigation of Councillor Boatman. This picture shows some of the crowds that visited the resort. Stage shows and band concerts were a popular attraction as were boat trips, paddling and crabbing. The *Exmouth* swimming bath can be seen to the right of centre on this card, postmarked 1913.

30.   One of the main attractions at Grays Beach was the bathing pond. Fitted with changing rooms and an array of diving boards at the deep end, it was always well patronised especially during school holidays. Originally water was fed into the pond by pipes laid out into the nearby Thames.

31.   Paddle steamer at Tilbury. A river crossing existed at Tilbury as far back as Roman times. One of the earliest written references is dated 1218 and concerns rent payments. Henry VIII's troops were ferried across here. In 1852 the London, Tilbury and Southend Railway was given rights to operate a steam ferry, which is now run by British Rail.

32. Fobbing Wharf in the days when it was still the base for 12 Thames barges. The barge pictured here is *Eliza of Rochester*. To the right of the tarred weather-boarded building the rear of the old *Ship Inn* can be seen. This card is postmarked 1908.

33. This picture, *c*.1910, shows a Thames barge at Stanford-le-Hope Wharf, probably taking on hay for horses in London. A barn bulging with hay can be seen just to the rear of the barge.

The Railway

The railway came to Thurrock in the late 1800s and rapidly opened up the area to development. The first railway company was the London, Tilbury & Southend which was incorporated in 1862. The lines ran across Thurrock from west to east, dipping down about half way to link up with the Tilbury to Gravesend Ferry. In 1880 the company took delivery of the first of its own engines – until then they had used locomotives loaned by the G.E.R. Many of the L.T.S.R.'s engines were named after towns and villages in Thurrock. The L.T.S.R. was taken over by the Midland Railway in 1912. The Corringham Light Railway connected Kynoch's explosives works to the L.T.S.R. in 1901.

34.   This postcard produced by W. R. Menlove shows the staff of Grays railway station. The badges on their caps identify two ticket examiners, two foremen and a guard plus of course the station cat. The date 28 September 1914 on the back of the card gives us an instant record of the staff at the beginning of the Great War.

35. A superb picture of Purfleet station on the London, Tilbury & Southend line. In the foreground are three horse-drawn carts heavily laden with dung removed from the quarry stables to the rear of the station. The entrance to Botany Gardens was a few yards behind where the photographer stood to take this picture, postmarked 1908.

36. South Ockendon railway station. The buildings on the left are still standing, as is the waiting room on the right. The old iron footbridge has been replaced and the signal box has been removed. The fields beyond the station now contain a council housing estate.

37.   A very early photograph of the Purfleet station when it was busy with daytrippers from London. They came down to Purfleet-on-Thames for the beach and Botany Gardens. The gardens were laid out in an old chalk quarry not far from the railway station.

38.   Grays railway station. This picture shows the up side (to London). It has now been completely rebuilt although the down side waiting room and ticket office have changed little. The carriage may perhaps be waiting for the master of one of the local 'big houses'.

32253. GRAYS RAILWAY STATION.

39.   Tilbury Town railway station. Situated in Dock Road and right outside the dock entrance, Tilbury Town station was known as the 'dockies station'. Still used by dock workers today, it also now sees many commuters on their way to London.

40.   Known as Tilbury Riverside, this has always been a very busy station. Up to the present day it has been a picking up point for the Tilbury to Gravesend ferry. P & O used the jetty adjacent to the station for many years as the point of embarkation for their Australian emigration run. Note the news sheets – one reads 'battle in the Soudan' dating the photograph to 1885.

41. Stanford-le-Hope railway station. In the early years of this century Stanford was a very rural area. The ladies in this picture, postmarked 1908, are still dressed in restricted Edwardian style, although one of them has stepped into the 20th century and rides a bicycle. The sign to the right is advertising '16 guinea pianos for 10/6 per month'.

42. Stanford-le-Hope level crossing in London Road. For a number of years this crossing never had gates but was closed off by means of a section of platform being wheeled across the gap. This can be seen on the extreme left. The engine, Number 36, is the *Walthamstow*.

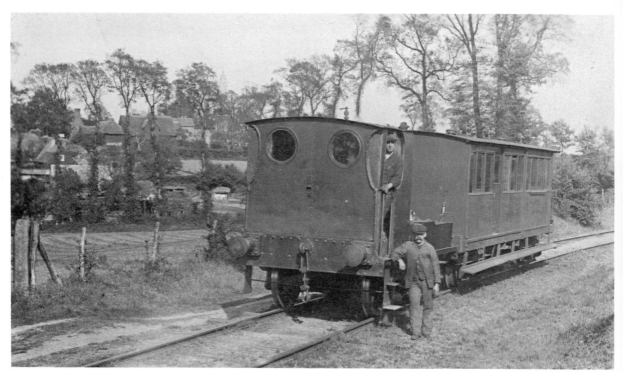

43.   Opened in 1901, the Corringham Light Railway was used to transport workers and supplies across the marshes to Kynoch's explosives factory. Two engines, the *Kynite* and *Cordite*, were used to haul the carriages from Corringham along the 2¾-mile track. The fare in 1901 was 1½d. The line closed in 1952.

44.   Many happy memories are associated with the hardworking engines that once ran from Fenchurch Street to Shoeburyness on the L.T.S.R. lines. The *Thames Haven* was built in 1881 and saw service with both L.T.S.R. and L.M.S. until September 1935 when she was withdrawn.

45. This engine, the No. 69 *Corringham*, was built in 1903 and was used to haul freight waggons. No. 69 gave many years of loyal service and was still working well into the 1940s. The destination board shows the route terminated at Tilbury Riverside for the Tilbury to Gravesend Ferry.

46. The *Thundersley* had quite a chequered career. She was built in 1909, named *Southend on Sea* and exhibited at the White City. Later she was renamed *Thundersley* and, elaborately decorated, was used to celebrate the Coronation of King George V in June 1911.

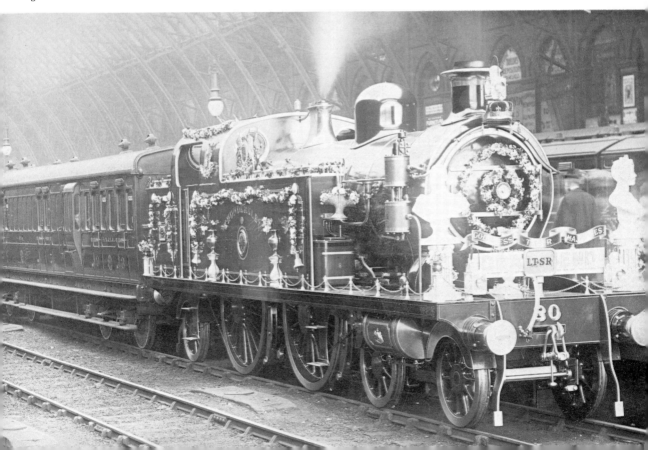

47. Another favourite on the local tracks was the *Aveley*. London, Tilbury & Southend Railway were very proud of their rolling stock and were strict as regards their cleanliness. This can be clearly seen in the shining paintwork and gleaming brass of this engine.

48. Hundreds of local people have affectionate memories of these Leyland buses that ran on the 370 route from Grays to Romford. Picking up at Grays war memorial, they threaded their way through North Stifford, the Ockendons, Upminster and Hornchurch. On Romford market days these buses were often packed to capacity.

Social Events

49. Parade in Clarence Road, Grays. The occasion is unknown – perhaps it was a parade to celebrate the end of the Great War. The names Everett, Davie, Cable and Ager are written on the back of the photograph and presumably identify the men sitting in the carriage.

50. Mrs. Dawson of Grays photographed just after she had won first prize in a hair competition at the Kursaal, Southend-on-Sea, 19 August 1908. Pictures and reports of this lady appeared in many national magazines and newspapers.

51. In November 1913 Grays virtually came to a standstill for the funeral of Mr. Charles Seabrooke who was head of the local Thorrock Brewery. In this picture the funeral procession is making its way down New Road, passing the *Grays & Tilbury Gazette* offices on its way to Grays parish church.

52. A charming study of boys at play. The bells had been removed from St Michael's church, Fobbing. The picture dates back to about 1930-31 when work was undertaken to rehang the bells in a new steel frame after the old bell frame had fallen into disrepair.

53. Grays Co-operative Society was set up in 1867, their first shop being the 'Old Dutch House' in the High Street. Well known local names appeared on the rules issued in 1866, amongst them Dines, Redington, Turp and Harris. This picture shows the Junior Co-op Guild parading in Grays High Street on Gala Day, 3 July 1921.

54. The aftermath of a fire at Corringham in February 1914. The whole family appears to be posing for the photographer on the still smoking ruins of their home. Note the line across the picture made by the cracked glass negative.

55.　Aveley High Street sometime before World War One. This picture shows a church parade being led by the local fire brigade. Further back in the parade groups are carrying banners which proclaim their allegiance to such societies as the Ancient Order of Foresters. Note the children's Sunday finery and the horse feeding from a nosebag.

CHADWELL ST MARY   UPPER WARD

56.   A superb picture of young children posing on Children's Day at Chadwell St Mary in 1906. The day consisted of games, competitions and a tea.

CHILDRENS DAY

ON STRIKE DUTY AT GRA

57. Grays railway station at the time of the dock strike in 1912. Police officers were drafted in from other forces to quell the unrest caused by 'blacklegs' working at the docks. Stories are still told about strike-breakers' trains being pelted as they passed through Grays on their way to Tilbury Docks.

TAKING JULY 1912

58. Moving a tree at Purfleet. A mature tree, standing some 40 feet high, has been dug up complete with root. Placed on a cart pulled by five horses, it was carried away from a site about to be redeveloped and replanted.

59. The first waterplane to land on Grays Beach. One old local remembers talk just before World War One of setting up a seaplane base at Grays, though it is not known whether this was for civil or military use.

Education

60. This picture was taken in the playground of Quarry Hill school in about 1920. It shows a group of schoolchildren dressed up for what could have been a Christmas show – it was certainly winter time, judging by the bare trees and traces of snow on the ground.

61. Opened in 1889, the Bridge Road schools were built on the floor of one of the worked out brickfields that pockmark this side of Grays. These schools took senior pupils from Quarry Hill and Arthur Street schools, now used for adult education classes. Note the pinafore dresses of the girls and the knickerbockers the boys are wearing.

62. Orsett School, a Church of England foundation, was built in 1848 for 102 girls and small boys, plus 66 infants. Education cost one penny a week for girls, two pence for infants and three pence for the whole family. Mr. J. Pattison is a fondly remembered headmaster who came to Orsett in 1931 and taught many generations.

63. Kynochtown housed workers employed at Kynoch's explosives factory. The school was opened in 1899. With the approach of World War One, the works grew rapidly and, in addition to the school, the village contained shops, a post office and an institute.

64. This postcard, produced about 1930, shows part of the Stepney Homes in North Stifford. Formerly used to house orphans from London, it was run as an approved school from the mid-1930s. Many local parents used to threaten to send their children here if they misbehaved. The establishment is now known as Ardale Community Home.

65. Early this century the teaching of religion was very important. Various religious bodies set up Sunday Schools and in this picture, postmarked 1906, we see the pupils of the Wesleyan Sunday School at Stanford-le-Hope. Photographed during a day out in the country, the pupils were perhaps studying the wonders of God and nature.

66. The schools and reading room at North Ockendon were opened in 1842 and enlarged in 1869 and 1892. By 1905, 90 local children were in attendance. The school log has some interesting entries; for instance, '4th October 1895. Rose Polley died this week of diphtheria' and in January 1944 it is recorded that the school was damaged by a bomb. It finally closed in 1980.

SCHOOLS & READING ROOM
N'TH OCKENDON

67.   West Thurrock school was opened in 1879 just nine years after Forster's Education Act was introduced. It replaced a Cottage School which had been run for a number of years by Mrs. Bobbett and her daughter. Like other rural schools, West Thurrock's registers show that many of its pupils were regularly absent for country activities like fruit and vegetable picking.

68.   Built by the Grays School Board and opened in January 1884, Quarry Hill School consisted of boys' and girls' schools with infants' departments. It was altered and enlarged many times to accommodate the growing population of Grays. In 1902 the headmaster received £180 p.a. plus a house, coal and light valued at £35. It is now the site of the police station.

69. Established in 1887, the Collegiate School was situated in Fairview Avenue, Stanford-le-Hope. An advertisement dated 1905 tells all: 'Pupils are prepared for London Matriculation and all public examinations. Every home care and comfort given to boarders of whom only a limited number are received. Very moderate terms.'

Sports and Pastimes

70.   A superb picture of the team that represented Tilbury Dock Police Football Club during their 1913-14 season. In the background are some of the buildings which once formed part of the now demolished Passmore Edwards Hospital.

71. Grays Athletic F.C. The first team is pictured here with managers and officials in front of the main stand at the Bridge Road ground in the 1921-22 season. The third amateur club to win the Dewar Shield in the Premier Division of the London League, beating Catford Southend, it ranked at that time with such clubs as Arsenal, Spurs, Chelsea, West Ham, Millwall and Fulham.

Season 1921-22.

Photo
S. Edwin.

72. Built in 1910, the Empire Theatre at Grays staged many fine shows with big stars of the time treading the boards. Perhaps the biggest was Marie Lloyd who came here in 1916. The Empire was later converted to show films, and spent its last days as a vegetable shop and supermarket.

73. Early this century cycling clubs were very popular. To cater for the cyclist, halts or rests were set up throughout the country. This one in London Road, Stanford-le-Hope, at Whitsun 1909 was obviously very popular and offered accommodation for cyclists, motorists and horses in addition to refreshments.

74. This postcard by W. R. Menlove shows Grays Cycle Club passing the school in East Thurrock Road, Grays, on their way to Tilbury to cross the Thames for Rainham in Kent in 1912. Menlove probably took the photograph from an upstairs window in his house which was in the road that can be seen bottom right.

75. Grays Park was a favourite venue for the Royal Pierrot Team. Organised by Albert P. Cross, they drew large crowds to their nightly performances. Local businessman A. Russell of Orsett Road, Grays, was quick to take advantage of publicity. He supplied the piano and stood an advertisement beside it to publicise himself.

76. Grays Temperance Silver Band, very smartly turned out and photographed in 1932 in front of the bandstand in Grays Park. The shield and cup in the foreground indicate that they must have just won a competition.

ER PRIZE BAND.   1932.

Essex Club & Ground

77.   A photograph taken at Grays Rec. at the end of the match between Essex Club and Ground and Grays Wednesday on 8 July 1914. The message on the back explains 'We got 213 for 7 wickets declared and Essex all out 100'.

Grays Wednesday 8-7-14

Shops and Businesses

78. A pre-First World War lorry owned by Redingtons, photographed in 'blood alley' behind their shop in Grays High Street. This alley ran from George Street to London Road and was so named because a butcher had a slaughter house there. The lorry is loaded with potatoes which explains the hand-written caption.

79. Before television was invented or radios were widely available, entertainment was home made. Most people were musically inclined and many homes had pianos. Sidney White's business at No. 41 Orsett Road, Grays, catered for the piano player by selling popular sheet music of the day as well as doing repairs.

80. Noad and Frank West. Noad's, which closed in 1981, once had four shops in New Road, Grays, and two shops in Orsett Road, selling furniture, cycles, records, pianos and prams. Frank West started off in New Road but moved to the High Street, becoming a highly respected men's and boys' outfitters.

81. Situated in the High Street within yards of the railway station and known as Central Premises, Grays Co-operative Society opened in 1884. The building housed the most modern of grocery stores with a covered arcade to the left. On the first floor was a short-lived tea rooms plus a reading room, library and offices. This picture is postmarked 1905.

82. A postcard of High Street, Grays, sent in 1913. Every business shown has now ceased trading. The clock marks Boatmans jewellers beside Bristow's Boot Warehouse, later Frank West. On the right is the Bon Marche Drapery Stores of Frank Spurr & Johnson. In the distance a barber's board announces 'haircuts 4d and shaves 6d'.

83. A close-up view of the Bon Marche Drapery Stores. Prices worth noting include painters' aprons 8d., youths' suits 13s.6d., men's suits 19s.6d., and ladies' straw hats 1s.11d.

84. The north end of Grays High Street. W. P. Walker's large ironmongers shop can be clearly seen with a fine array of goods outside. Westwood's tailors is next door, followed by George Carter's cycle stores and the Grays Pharmacy. McCarthy's Cash Chemist is on the extreme right.

85. Nelson's shop in New Road catered for Grays housewives who could buy a clothes mangle for 1s.6d. a week or a Normelle Radio for 4s. a week. The shop and houses were demolished during redevelopment.

86. Hall's Corner in the Broadway, Grays, about 60 years ago. It is now R. G. Coles' furniture shop. Hall's sold everything from boots at 4s. 11d. a pair to real cork linoleum at 2s. 6d. a yard. Customers travelled from far and wide to shop here. Note the extremely smart appearance of the staff.

87.   Formerly E. North's post office and cycle shop, this business in South Stifford began to cater for the early motorist. It was one of the first agents for Pratts Petroleum and the delivery hoses used to swing out across the path. Note the poster on the side wall advertising the Empire Theatre, Grays.

88.   Hill's Garage, Chadwell St Mary, on a card posted in 1937. A garage still stands on this site although it is now a modern service station. Prices on the pumps show a gallon of B.P. petrol cost 1s. 5d. whilst Power Ethyl was 1s. 7d. In addition to the garage, Hill had the shop next door selling cycles and accessories.

89. The Green, Stanford, in the early years of this century. The white building in the centre was the *Cock and Magpie Inn*, demolished in 1929 when it was over 300 years old. During the last century a fisherman died in this inn after being shot for trespassing at Shell Haven Creek. Local landowner Captain Moir was found guilty of murder and hanged.

90. Another view of the Green, showing its northern side and the top of the High Street. These businesses including Drayton Wright, publisher of this postcard, have now gone. His shop and photographer's studio is seen to the right of Horncastle's shop.

91. The post office at Stanford-le-Hope was located on the Green. In the early years of the century a letter could be sent to anywhere in the country for ½d. and the post office employed two postmen, a postmistress and a telegraph boy who can be seen on his bicycle in plate 89.

92. Thames Stores, Kynochtown. Here the workers at the munitions factory could buy all their daily needs including groceries, ironmongery, wines and spirits, and stamps. They would also have caught up on the local gossip.

93. An idyllic scene little changed today. The post office at Orsett was housed in the old Church House which stands opposite the church. Only recently losing its licence, it was run for many years by the Ridgwells, a well known Orsett family.

94. Grays High Street near the railway station was the site of this establishment. This card, postmarked 1906, is a superb record of the time when the temperance movement was strong. The window displays jars of biscuits, cakes and pastries and, of course, bottles of non-alcoholic drinks.

95. Taken around 1912, this picture shows C. Osborne's butcher's shop at No. 5 Clarence Road, Grays. At one time most butchers displayed their meat in this way. The photograph, taken early on a Saturday morning, shows beef and pig carcasses ready to be cut into Sunday joints.

Public Houses

Many of Thurrock's public houses were owned by Seabrooke & Sons who ran the famous Thorrock Brewery. Seabrooke's brewery was situated close to the river in Grays where it had other interests including a fleet of Thames barges and a coal merchant business. Over the last few years many of the older public houses, particularly in Grays, have been lost.

96.   The *Plough*, South Ockendon, formerly a Seabrooke's house. The cottages on the left have now been demolished and replaced by new houses. The cart shed attached to the cottages was used for a number of years as a cycle shop and garage. More recently it was an off-licence but it has since been demolished.

97.   The *Ship*, West Thurrock, also formerly one of Seabrooke's long line of public houses. It was for many years popular with seamen who visited the various wharves along the Thames just a few hundred yards from the public house in London Road. This photograph was taken in the early 1950s.

98. The *Fox & Goose*, West Thurrock. Owned by Ind Coope of Romford, this inn was built in the once rural West Thurrock. A firm favourite with local farm workers, it was also the headquarters of the West Thurrock Cycle Club and the local branch of the Ancient Order of Foresters. Note the horse trough, another reminder of a more leisurely age.

99. The *Railway Hotel*, Grays. Named to commemorate the coming of the railway to Grays, it was built in the manner typical of many of Seabrooke's houses. There were once livery stables beyond the coach arch seen on the right. This picture was taken just prior to the First World War.

100.   A view of part of Grays that has now gone, the Old High Street was a mass of weather-boarded buildings. The *White Hart* is on the left, facing the *Anchor & Hope*. Both houses were much frequented by seamen and legend states they were the haunt of smugglers.

101.   The top end of the Old High Street, Grays, showing the now demolished *Kings Arms Hotel*. Standing next to the market square, it was a favourite with shoppers and stallholders alike. On the right is the *Rising Sun*, a public house run for many years by Mr. & Mrs. Sims.

102.   The *Queen's Hotel*, Grays. Built by Seabrooke's in 1888 at a cost of £7,000, there was great excitement there in 1890 when a fire broke out. Grays fire brigade controlled the blaze but much of the building was damaged. The *Queen's* stood in the High Street at its junction with Orsett and Clarence Roads, but was demolished during redevelopment of the area.

103.   The *Half Moon*, Little Thurrock. This public house was built in the Broadway by Thorrock Brewery. Photographed just before the First World War, a row of shops can be seen to the right of the *Half Moon*. These were originally houses built by Seabrooke's for their employees.

104. A few hundred yards beyond the *Half Moon* in Little Thurrock was the *Ship Inn*, now replaced by a more modern building. The one shown here belonged to the Old Hornchurch Brewery, a rival of Seabrooke's. Note the horse trough the boys are leaning against.

105. A busy scene in Dock Road, Tilbury, *c*.1910. The *Ship Hotel*, situated close to the dock entrance, was popular with dockers and seamen. In addition to the usual bars, it had a coffee and billiard room. The number of men hanging around the building suggests that opening time may be close at hand.

106. *Tilbury Hotel* from the river. Opened in 1886, it was destroyed by fire in 1944 after being bombed. A description on the back of the postcard reads, 'The Tilbury Hotel is most pleasantly situated in its own charming grounds on the north bank of the Thames opposite Gravesend and from its windows may be witnessed an attractive panorama of shipping unequalled in any other port in the world.'

107. *Basin Tavern*, Tilbury. Looking more like a mansion than a public house, this fine looking building owned by Truman, Hanbury, Buxton & Co. has long since been demolished.

108. The *Rising Sun*, Stanford-le-Hope, owned by the Stanford brewers Blyth & Squier. It was taken over by Seabrooke's in 1913. Note the barmaids at the door and the drayman about to make a delivery.

109. The *Old Bull*, Corringham. Photographed at the time when James Lester held the licence, it was built over 500 years ago and has altered little over the years. It is believed to have been the haunt of smugglers, and secret panels and chambers have been found. The market and annual fair were once held in front of the *Bull*, and the stocks stood close by the church wall.

110. The *Haven Hotel*, Coryton, which was built amongst the oil refineries where once Kynoch's explosives factory stood. The hotel's main purpose was to cater for workers and visitors who came to the various plants at Coryton and Thames Haven.

111. Standing at the top of the hill leading from Corringham to Fobbing, the *White Lion* is an imposing 15th-century building. The structure to the right of the main building was once used for stabling, but later in the era of the Thames barge it was a sail loft where sails were made and repaired.

Fobbing

The Old Ship Inn.

112. Situated beside Fobbing creek, the *Old Ship* was an inn for over 200 years. It was owned by the Crown Brewery of Billericay and is thought to have been the inspiration for Charles Dickens when he wrote Magwitch's escape scene in *Great Expectations*.

113. The *Whitmore Arms*, Orsett. Once the site of the *George* and later the *Dog & Gun*, the *Whitmore Arms* commemorates the fact that Col. Sir Francis Whitmore, once Lord Lieutenant of Essex, lived at Orsett Hall. The public footpath that runs down beside the inn is known locally as Gunn Alley.

114.   The *Royal Oak*, South Ockendon. This 15th-century timber-framed farm house was known as 'Eldertons' during the reign of Charles II. It has also been called Finch's Farm and was the home of the Benton family. Over the years it became a beer house.

115.   *Dock House Hotel*, Thames Haven, was another Seabrooke's house, built on Thames Haven marshes to cater for bargees and workers at the nearby wharf. Near this house was the site of the bare knuckle heavyweight championship in November 1862 between Jem Mace and Tom King. Tom King was declared the winner in the 20th round.

116. The *Bricklayers Arms*, Grays. This public house, one of Seabrooke & Sons', is on the corner of Bridge Road and William Street. It was a favourite drinking place for men working in the local brickfields. Jack Golden held the licence for many years and can be seen in this picture (elbow on windowsill) flanked by his staff.

Thurrock at War

A number of army camps and military sites were established in Thurrock, the most famous being Purfleet Camp. Many soldiers either passed through Thurrock or were stationed here to guard important strategic places such as Tilbury Docks, oil refineries and industrial establishments.

"I'm Thinking of YOU Everyday."

At PURFLEET CAMP. —— *A Soldier's Letter*

I haven't had time to sit down and write,
    And thought perhaps you might grieve ;
So I send you this card just to say I'm alright,
    And longing to see you again when on "leave."

When the Empire's Call for more men to fight,
    For her Honour—in me caused a thrill;
I felt fight I must or else I should "bust,"
    So I'm at PURFLEET Camp —hard at drill.

The work it is stiff for we're "at it" all day,
    And sometimes half of the night ;
But we're hardening to it and getting quite fit,
    And thank goodness for "grub" we're alright.

My duty calls me as this picture shows,
    To the Front where the fightin' is done ;
And when *Purfleet Camp Boys* get grip on the foe,
    There's no letting go till they've won.

So cheer up, my dear, tho' parted we are,
    And though I'm so far away ;
My loved ones are ever *first* in my thoughts,
    I'm thinking of YOU *everyday.*

From _____ At _____

At " Duty's Call."

117. A postcard sent by Rifleman A. Higgins of Purfleet Camp to his girlfriend in Bow, East London, in 1917. He has written that he is leaving Purfleet Camp and hopes to see her soon and says 'I am sorry to hear about your friends troubles of losing their chaps. I expect it was a swipe to you all.'

Incendiary Bombs found "somewhere in England"

118. A wonderful close-up picture of World War One incendiary bombs which have obviously done their intended job and been recovered from the ground. Due to censorship, the postcard has had to be captioned 'somewhere in England' but fortunately someone has written on the back, 'Dropped near Aveley during the Great War 1914-18'.

119. In addition to the camp at Purfleet, Thurrock had a number of other military establishments especially at strategic points such as the docks and oil refineries. This picture shows a group of London electrical engineers who were stationed at Thames Haven in 1915.

L.E.E.s Thames Haven. Det. 1915.

120.   A fine study by Mr. Menlove of an expectant crowd outside the Grays Unionist Club in Orsett Road. They are waiting for Kitchener's Volunteers who were on their way to Grays railway station in March 1916. T.S. *Exmouth's* band leads the parade. A poster on the wall reads 'Single men. Last days of voluntary enlistment. Last day March – '.

121.   A military funeral at Grays, October 1916. Another photograph by Mr. Menlove which shows the other side of the war story. Here we see one of the unfortunate volunteers just seven months after the photograph above was taken. His name is unknown, but boys from one of the training ships were used to pull his coffin mounted on a gun carriage.

122.   When World War One finished funds were set up all over the country to finance the erection of memorials to commemorate those who died fighting for freedom. Grays war memorial was set up in front of the old police station and unveiled by the Lord Lieutenant of Essex, witnessed by a huge crowd, on 6 March 1921.

123.   'A passing out group sometime between 1939 and 1945', photographed at Purfleet Camp. Note the tape on the windows of the huts in the background to prevent the glass falling out if it was broken by a bomb blast.

Miscellany

124. Parts of Belhus Lodge in Aveley date back to the 16th century. It was once the home of the Barrett-Lennards. Note the thatched roof summer house in the foreground. During World War Two the house was used to billet soldiers and was much mistreated by them and later vandalised. It was demolished in 1956.

125. South Ockendon village some 70 years ago. Since then all the shops on the left hand side have been demolished. Boreham's the bakers had some fine enamel signs on their wall; next door was the village sweet shop, a firm favourite with the children who attended the school just round the corner.

126.   Aveley village 80 years ago. The girls are standing on the junction of High Street, Mill Lane and Purfleet Road. A garage now stands on the site of the thatched cottage in the foreground and the other houses have also been demolished.

127.   Once known as Purfleet-on-Thames, trippers came here much as they go to Southend today. To cater for them, refreshment rooms were opened: Cox and Palmer's tea garden was one such establishment. It was situated on the green at the water's edge, adjacent to the *Royal Hotel*.

128. West Thurrock lighthouse was one of a number of lights set up in the mid-1800s by Trinity House as an aid to navigation in the Thames. Positioned on bends and standing some 30-40 feet high, these lights could be seen for miles.

129. West Thurrock vicarage, a well-built house which stood in London Road not far from what remains of the old village. It has now been demolished. This card was postmarked 1908.

130. Pilgrims Lane in North Stifford, also known as Davey Down, was once used by hundreds of pilgrims on their way to Thomas à Becket's shrine at Canterbury. The now demolished cottages on the left were the Poor's Cottages and that on the right which still stands was once an inn.

131. The now demolished premises of J. W. Pigg & Sons. The site, known as Pigg's Corner, contained a grocery shop, offices and garages as well as a large modern bakery. Pigg's once had shops all over Thurrock and operated a delivery service that was second to none. The site now houses an old people's complex.

132. The High Street, Grays, photographed in the days before the one-way system and precinct were thought of. A local bus waits outside the now demolished *Queen's Hotel*. Opposite, a six-wheeled double decker bound for Purfleet stands outside such shops as International Stores, Liptons and G. Lyndon Rhodes, the well known local men's outfitters. This card is postmarked 1930.

133. Dell Road, Grays, was once only a lane leading to farm land, with few houses. Dell Lodge, now demolished, was one of them. Beside the house a drive led to The Dell, built in 1872 by Alfred Russell Wallace who once worked with Charles Darwin. Dell Lodge was Wallace's gate-keeper's house.

134. The Free Library, Grays, designed by Christopher M. Shiner and opened on 11 November 1903. American philanthropist Andrew Carnegie gave £3,000 for its erection and donations from local schoolchildren bought the clock. It was demolished in 1970 to the consternation of local people.

135.   The fire station in Grays stood almost opposite the library in Orsett Road. Opened in 1893, it, too, was designed by local architect Christopher M. Shiner and was the headquarters of Grays fire brigade for many years.

136. The police station in Grays stood where the law courts now stand. Its position was such that from its windows the whole High Street could be seen. In the days before Grays had a police station, prisoners were conveyed to Orsett where they were incarcerated until they could be taken to Chelmsford for trial. The building has now been demolished.

137.   Rook Hall, Dell Road, Grays. Built during Victoria's reign on the floor of an old brickfield, it was named after a large rookery which once flourished in the woods to the rear. William Wright a local farmer owned the house for many years and farmed most of the land in the area early this century. The house has now been demolished.

138.   The Methodist church in London Road, Grays, was built in 1885 at a cost of £2,600. It could seat 406. Before its erection, meetings were held in Quarry Hill School. A gallery should have gone all round the interior but only one side was completed, and the stairs were never built. The basement contained classrooms. The church was demolished in 1986.

139. Sleepers Farm, Chadwell St Mary, with a thatched barn to the left. The house can be dated back to the 15th century and looks as splendid today as when this picture was taken some 70 years ago.

140. Hundreds of ships came into Tilbury Dock and the risk of a crew member falling ill was great. To combat this Tilbury Hospital was built. This photograph shows the new ward for Indian patients opened by the Duke of York in 1924. On the back of the postcard is written 'Tilbury Girl Guides went on guard of honour'.

141. Tilbury grew rapidly once the docks were opened and many rows of houses were built to accommodate the workers. This picture shows one of those houses in Peninsular Road. Standing at the gate are Mr. Webb and his family – Mr. Webb was the dry dock foreman.

142. Before the days of piped water the only way to get fresh water was from a street pump. This example was situated in Pump Street in Horndon and commemorated Queen Victoria's 1887 Jubilee. The lower spout was for filling buckets, the trough was for horses and the higher spout was for filling a cart that toured the area selling water.

143. East Tilbury Rectory. Built in the late 18th century, this fine house once stood right at the entrance to the village, with the church at the other extreme. From its windows there were magnificent views: from the front West Tilbury and its church, and from the back the Thames snaking its way to the sea.

144. Poor Houses in Fobbing Road, Corringham. These are thought to date back to the 16th century and were used by the Charity Commission in the 19th century to provide an income to purchase fuel and food for the local poor. They were bought in 1914 for £300 by blacksmith John Ransom and demolished in 1931.

145. In the closing years of the 19th century the Wesleyan movement was very strong in Thurrock and chapels were opened throughout the area. This one at Fobbing was opened in 1887, Queen Victoria's Golden Jubilee year.

146. The Bottle House, Fobbing, was a fine red brick Georgian building in Wharf Road. During its construction the bases of bottles had been pushed into the plaster as decoration. During demolition in the early 1950s workmen found a number of bricked-up doors.

147.   Pictures of the hamlet of Baker Street are rare. This photograph is only 25-30 years old but changes have occurred since it was taken. The most significant is the loss of the cottages on the left. Two rows stood along the raised pavement, namely Lindseys and Saunders. Lindseys Cottages belonged to the family which worked Baker Street Mill.

148.   Now the site of Orsett Hospital, this was once the local workhouse. Many local residents can remember the original buildings such as the lodge at the gatehouse and the dormitories with their flagstone floors. This card is postmarked 1910.

149. Belmont Castle, Grays, which was built in 1795 for Zachariah Button. The grounds of this house were beautifully landscaped and contained many fine cedar trees as well as ornamental hedges. From windows on the south side, fine views of the hills of Kent could be seen. The 'castle' was demolished in 1943 to make way for quarries.

150. Work on building the docks at Tilbury began in the 1880s. To accommodate the many hundreds of dockers who would be employed, blocks of flats or dwellings as they were known were built. Although drab to look at, they were considered to be the most modern housing of the time. They were demolished in the 1950s.

151.   This greetings card from Grays, posted in 1907, uses the 'multiple technique' and shows views of tourist spots – the library, park, beach, High Street and Palmers College.

152.   Purfleet and Stanford-le-Hope also produced 'seaside postcards'. This example is postmarked July 1912.

153.   A Christmas greeting postcard from Purfleet.

154.   The smaller inland villages of Thurrock as well as the seaside resorts produced greetings cards.

155. A multiple view card of Stifford.

156. A New Year card sent from Corringham in 1907.

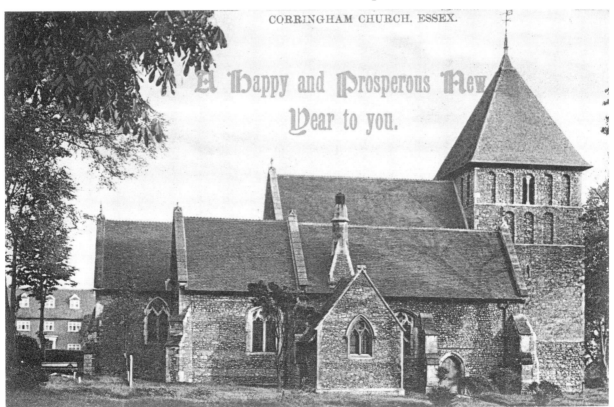

157. & 158. (opposite) Harris's coaches have a long and respected tradition in Thurrock. These examples were owned by the firm in the early 1950s. *Above* is a Leyland, possibly parked behind Dreamland at Margate, a favourite holiday destination of the time. *Below* is a Bedford. On the radiator grille an early A.A. badge and a badge for the Bedford Drivers' Club are displayed. Both coaches have radio aerials.

Travel by Coach - - - *Travel in Comfort*

HARRIS'S COACHES

Latest luxury type coaches may be hired at reasonable rates

25, 27, 29 SEATERS ANYWHERE—ANYTIME 32, 33, 35 SEATERS

Write or Call: 8 PARKER ROAD, GRAYS

PHONE: TILBURY 212.   SPECIALISTS IN PRIVATE HIRE

159. The advertisement printed on the back of plate 157.

160.   Another favourite day out was to take a boat trip. This picture shows the *Royal Eagle* calling at Tilbury Pier. This old paddle steamer toured the Thames and Medway in the 1930s.

161.   The next two postcards were sold to aid fund raising. Both were used to raise money for the Passmore Edwards' District Cottage Hospital in Tilbury. This card shows R.M.S. *Marmora* which was owned by P & O who put it on exhibition in 1903.

Match Oct. 14th., 1916
Kynochtown

Arranged by
Y. LATE

Written by
Percy Verance
and Y. NOTT.

Kynoch's Knockouts

SOME FOOTBALL TEAM

(Parody on " The Broken Doll."

I'M fond of sport and so I thought
                    The other day,
I'd go and see our Kynoch boys
                    At Football play.
They'd made arrangements with the soldiers
                    O'er the way,
To have a friendly game
                    Upon that Saturday

Chorus—They made the kick-off just for 3-15,
         The R.E. Band was playing on the green
      The Suffolks shaped well but I must confess
      That owing to the wind it placed them all
                              in a mess.
      The people cheered as Kynoch's scored first
                              goal
         They shortly added second to the roll,
      The ' winger' made it three, but I lost my £.s.d.
      And went back home—"A Broken Doll."

Proceeds on 300
to Tilbury Hospital.

1d. Per Copy

162. This card advertised a football match in October 1916 at Kynochtown, one team being Kynoch's Knockouts. Each card was sold for 1d. and the money raised by the sale of 300 went to the hospital.

163.   Postcards were be a very good vehicle for carrying advertisements. This one was produced by a watch and clock repairer who traded in Fobbing around 1910. Mr. Spunner issued these cards to advertise his services which included the repair and tuning of pianos and organs.

164.   This shop is thought to have been in the Old High Street, Grays. Two very smart and proud young men stand beside a fantastic window display. The shop is obviously a barber's because of the striped pole on the door post but the window displays the wares of photographer, Frank Holbrook.

165. This 1920s photograph has been included to show that some of the buildings in Tilbury are slowly sinking into the marshland on which they were built early in the century. It shows the shops in Civic Square soon after they were built, standing at normal road level. Today one has to descend a number of steps to reach their front doors.

166. A rare early aerial photograph showing Tilbury Dock in the early 1920s. Towards the top of the picture can be seen The Dwellings with the old Tilbury Hospital to the right. At the very top of the photograph is the nucleus of the Tilbury housing estate.

167. A photograph representing Queen Elizabeth I's visit to Tilbury in 1588, taken at an Aldershot Tattoo. This book is published in 1988, the 400th anniversary of that visit at the time of the threatened invasion by the Spanish Armada.